Greatest Ever

Cookies

The All Time Top 20 Greatest Recipes

Greatest Ever

Cookies

The All Time Top 20 Greatest Recipes

p

This is a Parragon Book
First published in 2002

Parragon
Queen Street House
4 Queen Street
Bath BA1 1HE, UK

ISBN: 0-75256-848-5

Printed in China

NOTE

This book uses metric and imperial measurements. Follow the same
units of measurement throughout; do not mix metric and imperial.
All spoon measurements are level: teaspoons are assumed to be 5 ml,
and tablespoons are assumed to be 15 ml. Unless otherwise stated,
milk is assumed to be full fat, eggs and individual vegetables such as
potatoes are medium, and pepper is freshly ground black pepper.

The times given for each recipe are an approximate guide only because
the preparation times may differ according to the techniques used by
different people and the cooking times may vary as a result of the type
of oven used. The preparation times include the chilling and marinating
times, where appropriate.

Recipes using raw or very lightly cooked eggs should be
avoided by infants, the elderly, pregnant women, convalescents,
and anyone suffering from an illness.

CONTENTS

VARIATIONS ON A THEME

Generally, cookie mixtures are much more robust than cake mixtures. In some cases, you can treat the recipe as a simple base for carrying other ingredients without upsetting the final result. In the Chewy Cherry Flapjacks, for example, you could substitute an equal quantity of chopped nuts, toasted sunflower seeds or raisins for the glacé cherries.

INTRODUCTION

It only takes one bite of a home-baked cookie to appreciate just how much crumblier and tastier it is than most of the biscuits you can buy ready made – and you can eat it while it's still warm.

As a snack food, cookies are very convenient. They are a quick source of carbohydrates, and are useful for topping up energy levels during the day. Using wholemeal flour instead of white flour in cookie recipes gives the finished product added fibre, which helps to keep the digestive system healthy.

Cookies are very straightforward to make – quick and easy to mix and cook. As a bonus, you can enjoy the tempting mouthwatering aromas coming from the oven while a tray of cookies is baking. Just be warned – once you have started stocking your biscuit tin with your home-made cookies, no-one is going to let you stop!

Above: Home-baked cookie recipes are very versatile – you can choose your favourite ingredients. Try using different types of dried fruits to make your own recipes unique.

MAKING COOKIES

Clear, step-by-step instructions will guide you through the measuring, mixing and baking of each recipe. Baking cookies does not call for the same precision as cake baking but there are still some ground rules to follow:

★ Make sure you read the recipe from start to finish so you know what ingredients you need.

★ Weigh out all the ingredients accurately and do any preparation, such as grating, chopping or tin lining before you start mixing.

★ Always use the size and shape of tin recommended in the recipe, otherwise the cookies may not cook properly in the time allowed.

★ Towards the end of the recommended baking time, check the cookies – generally they should be an even golden colour on top and slightly browner round the edges where the mixture is thinner.

★ Leave cookies on the baking sheet to cool slightly before transferring to a wire rack to finish cooling. Mark out the cutting lines on flapjacks after the initial period of cooling, as the mixture is much easier to cut at that stage.

★ Allow plenty of room between cookies on the baking sheet, especially those that are spooned on, as they have a tendency to spread out during baking.

raisins

nuts

All these cookies or traybakes are made from the simplest store-cupboard ingredients – flour, butter, eggs, sugar, rolled oats or popular breakfast cereals. Their flavours are easily pepped up with other dry ingredients, such as spices, chocolate, citrus zest, nuts, seeds and dried fruits.

cranberries

oranges

STORE-CUPBOARD

Chocolate

Used in moderation, chocolate chips or chunks of chocolate add a popular flavour to cookies. Melted chocolate can be used to decorate cookies.

Citrus zest

The finely grated zest of lemons, oranges or limes gives cookies a wonderful zing. Finely chopped candied peel provides chewy interest.

eggs

white chocolate

raspberries

Dried fruits

Raisins, sultanas and currants add a moist chewiness. Chopped glacé cherries and ready-to-eat apricots are also good cookie fodder. Do not use fresh fruit in cookie making as the juices released as the fruit softens will spoil the crispness.

Eggs

Sometimes an egg is used to bind the cookie mixture.

Fat

Although you can use margarine, butter gives the cookies a better, richer flavour. Before mixing, allow the butter to soften to room temperature so that it blends easily with the other ingredients.

lemons

Flour

Generally, plain white flour is used for making cookies, unless otherwise indicated in the recipe. You could use wholemeal plain flour instead to add more texture and flavour, but expect a slightly heavier result.

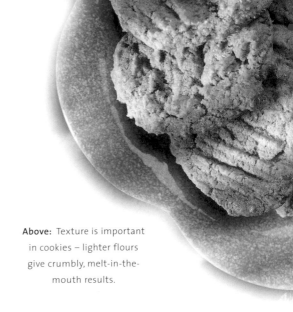

Above: Texture is important in cookies – lighter flours give crumbly, melt-in-the-mouth results.

Nuts

Chopped nuts – pecan nuts, walnuts, almonds, hazelnuts, peanuts and pistachios – add extra crunch and flavour. Grated coconut also adds excellent texture and taste.

Oatmeal

Ordinary rolled oats used for making porridge give flapjacks and oaty biscuits a rough, chewy texture.

Seeds

For wholesome cookies add sesame, sunflower, poppy and pumpkin seeds to the dough. Toast the seeds lightly first for greater flavour.

Spices

Regular baking spices, such as cinnamon, ginger and nutmeg are frequently used to flavour cookie dough. Good quality vanilla essence helps to bring out all the cookie's flavours and spicy aromas.

cinnamon sticks

Sugar

Coarser granulated sugar gives cookies a crunchier texture than fine caster sugar. Demerara and soft brown sugars add more colour and flavour.

dates

cocoa powder

figs

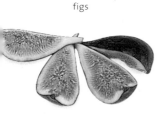

flour

Another nice thing about cookie baking is that you don't need much special equipment. You can usually mix the ingredients in a mixing bowl with a wooden spoon. Then you either bake the cookie mixture in several batches or use a couple of baking sheets so you can cook all the cookies at the same time.

cake tins

E Q U I P M E N T

wooden spoon

scraper

Baking sheets

It's worth spending a little more on buying two good quality baking sheets. These should have a thickish base which transfers the heat to the bottom of the cookies evenly and does not buckle in the oven. A non-stick surface makes removing the cookies easier but is not essential. You can always line an ordinary baking sheet with non-stick baking parchment.

Baking trays

You will need a 30 x 23-cm/ 12 x 9-inch baking tray for cooking flapjacks.

Cake tins

You need a 20-cm/8-inch shallow round cake tin for

baking a shortbread round. For traybakes, you need various shallow cake tins – 18-cm/7-inch, 20-cm/8-inch and 23-cm/9-inch squares.

Cookie cutters

For recipes in which the cookie dough is rolled out thinly, you need a cookie or scone cutter to stamp out the discs or shapes. Cookie cutters come in many different shapes and sizes from kitchen departments and cookery utensil shops. There are round, square, heart-shaped or novelty designs with plain or fluted edges – the choice is yours. Just bear in mind that if you alter the shape or size of the cutter recommended in the recipe, it will change the number of cookies you can expect to get out of each batch of dough.

scales

Cooling rack

Cookies should be cooled on a wire-mesh tray. Choose one with quite closely spaced rungs so the warm cookies cannot sag through the gaps.

Fish slice

The same fish slice you use for lifting fried eggs out of a pan can be used to transfer cookies from baking tray to cooling rack.

fish slice

Rolling pin

Some cookie mixtures are pressed into a baking tray and others are spooned on to baking sheets in free-form mounds. For others you will need a rolling pin to roll the dough out thinly.

Saucepan

For melted mixtures, such as flapjacks, you need a saucepan. Alternatively, you can melt liquid ingredients in a bowl in a microwave oven. In both cases, do not let the mixture get too hot.

rolling pins

mixing bowls

cake tin

baking sheet

pastry cutters

DARK CHOCOLATE CHIP & VANILLA COOKIES

>Makes 18   >Preparation time: 35 minutes   >Cooking time: 10–12 minutes

INGREDIENTS

175 g/6 oz plain flour

1 tsp baking powder

125 g/4½ oz soft margarine

90 g/3 oz light muscovado sugar

60 g/2 oz caster sugar

1/2 tsp vanilla essence

1 egg

125 g/4½ oz dark chocolate chips

METHOD

1 Lightly grease 2 baking trays.

2 Place all of the ingredients in a large mixing bowl and beat until well combined.

3 Place tablespoonfuls of the mixture on to the baking trays, spacing them well apart to allow for spreading during cooking.

4 Bake in a preheated oven, 190°C/375°F/Gas Mark 5, for 10–12 minutes, or until the cookies are golden brown.

5 Using a palette knife, transfer the cookies to a wire rack to cool completely.

BUTTER SHORTBREAD WEDGES

▸Makes 8   ▸Preparation time: 40 minutes   ▸Cooking time: 30–35 minutes

INGREDIENTS

125 g/4½ oz butter, softened

3 tbsp granulated sugar

2 tbsp icing sugar

225 g/8 oz plain flour

pinch of salt

2 tsp orange flower water

caster sugar, for sprinkling

METHOD

1 Lightly grease a 20-cm/8-inch shallow round cake tin.

2 In a large mixing bowl, cream together the butter, granulated sugar and icing sugar until light and fluffy.

3 Sieve the flour and salt into the mixture. Add the orange flower water and bring everything together to form a soft dough.

4 On a lightly floured surface, roll out the dough to a 20-cm/8-inch round and place in the tin. Prick the dough well and score into 8 triangles with a round-bladed knife.

5 Bake in a preheated oven, 150°C/300°F/Gas Mark 2, for 30–35 minutes, or until the biscuit is pale golden and crisp.

6 Sprinkle with caster sugar, then cut along the marked lines to make the wedge shapes.

7 Leave the shortbread to cool before removing it from the tin. Store in an airtight container.

CHEWY CHERRY FLAPJACKS

>Makes 16 >Preparation time: 45 minutes >Cooking time: 30 minutes

INGREDIENTS

200 g/7 oz butter

200 g/7 oz demerara sugar

2 tbsp golden syrup

275 g/9½ oz porridge oats

100 g/3½ oz desiccated coconut

75 g/2¼ oz glacé cherries, chopped

METHOD

1 Lightly grease a 30 x 23 cm/12 x 9 inch baking tray.

2 Heat the butter, demerara sugar and golden syrup in a large saucepan until just melted.

3 Stir in the oats, desiccated coconut and glacé cherries and mix well until evenly combined.

4 Spread the mixture on to the baking tray and press down with the back of a palette knife to make a smooth surface.

5 Bake in a preheated oven, 160°C/325°F/Gas Mark 3, for about 30 minutes.

6 Remove from the oven and leave to cool on the baking tray for about 10 minutes.

7 Cut the flapjack mixture into strips using a sharp knife.

8 Carefully transfer the flapjacks to a wire rack and leave to cool completely.

CHOCOLATE RICE SQUARES

>Makes 16 >Preparation time: 45 minutes >Cooking time: 5–10 minutes

INGREDIENTS

WHITE LAYER

4 tbsp butter

1 tbsp golden syrup

150 g/5½ oz white chocolate

50 g/1¾ oz toasted rice cereal

DARK LAYER

4 tbsp butter

2 tbsp golden syrup

125 g/4½ oz dark chocolate, broken into small pieces

75 g/2¾ oz toasted rice cereal

METHOD

1 Grease a 20-cm/8-inch square cake tin and line with baking paper.

2 To make the white chocolate layer, melt the butter, golden syrup and chocolate in a bowl set over a saucepan of gently simmering water.

3 Remove from the heat and stir in the rice cereal until it is well combined.

4 Press the mixture into the prepared tin and level the surface.

5 To make the dark chocolate layer, melt the butter, golden syrup and dark chocolate in a bowl set over a pan of gently simmering water.

6 Remove from the heat and stir in the rice cereal until it is well coated. Spread the dark chocolate layer over the white chocolate layer and chill until both layers have hardened.

7 Turn out of the cake tin and cut into 16 small squares, using a sharp knife.

SWEET HAZELNUT PASTRIES

>Makes about 26   >Preparation time: 15 minutes   >Cooking time: 10–15 minutes

INGREDIENTS

375 g/13 oz ready-made puff pastry

8 tbsp chocolate hazelnut spread

50 g/1¾ oz chopped toasted hazelnuts

5 tsp caster sugar

METHOD

1 Lightly grease a baking tray. On a lightly floured surface, roll out the puff pastry to a rectangle of about 38 x 23 cm/15 x 9 inches.

2 Spread the chocolate hazelnut spread over the pastry using a palette knife, then scatter the chopped hazelnuts over the top.

3 Roll up one long side of the pastry to the centre, then roll up the other side so that they meet in the centre. Where the pieces meet, dampen the edges with a little water to join them. Using a sharp knife, cut into thin slices. Place each slice on to the prepared baking tray and flatten slightly with a palette knife. Sprinkle the slices with the caster sugar.

4 Bake in a preheated oven, 220°C/425°F/Gas Mark 7, for about 10–15 minutes, or until golden. Transfer to a wire rack to cool.

RAISIN & CHERRY MORSELS

>Makes 8 >Preparation time: 15–20 minutes >Cooking time: 15–20 minutes

INGREDIENTS

200 g/7 oz plain flour

2 tsp baking powder

100 g/3½ oz butter, cut into small pieces

75 g/2¾ oz demerara sugar

100 g/3½ oz sultanas

2 tbsp glacé cherries, finely chopped

1 egg, beaten

2 tbsp milk

METHOD

1 Lightly grease a baking tray.

2 Sieve the flour and baking powder into a bowl. Rub in the butter with your fingers until the mixture resembles breadcrumbs.

3 Stir in the sugar, sultanas and glacé cherries.

4 Add the beaten egg and the milk to the mixture and mix to form a soft dough.

5 Spoon 8 mounds of the mixture on to the baking tray, spacing them well apart to allow for spreading during cooking.

6 Bake in a preheated oven, 200°C/400°F/Gas Mark 6, for 15–20 minutes, or until firm to the touch when pressed with a finger.

7 Remove from the baking tray. Either serve piping hot from the oven or transfer to a wire rack and leave to cool before serving.

CREAMY CARAMEL & OAT SQUARES

>Makes 16 >Preparation time: 40 minutes >Cooking time: 25 minutes

INGREDIENTS

100 g/3½ oz soft margarine

4 tbsp light muscovado sugar

125 g/4½ oz plain flour

40 g/1½ oz rolled oats

CARAMEL FILLING

25 g/1 oz butter

25 g/1 oz light muscovado sugar

200 ml/7 fl oz canned condensed milk

TOPPING

100 g/3½ oz dark chocolate

25 g/1 oz white chocolate, optional

METHOD

1 Beat together the margarine and muscovado sugar in a bowl until light and fluffy. Beat in the flour and rolled oats. Use your fingertips to bring the mixture together, if necessary.

2 Press the mixture into the base of a shallow 20-cm/8-inch square cake tin.

3 Bake in a preheated oven, 180°C/350°F/Gas Mark 4, for 25 minutes, or until just golden and firm. Cool in the tin.

4 Place the ingredients for the caramel filling in a pan and heat gently, stirring, until the sugar has dissolved and the ingredients combine. Bring to the boil over a very low heat, then boil gently for 3–4 minutes, stirring constantly until thickened.

5 Pour the caramel filling over the biscuit base in the tin and leave to set.

6 For the topping, melt the dark chocolate and spread it over the caramel. If using the white chocolate, melt it and pipe lines of white chocolate over the dark chocolate. Using a cocktail stick or a skewer, feather the white chocolate into the dark chocolate. Leave to set. Cut into squares to serve.

DARK CHOCOLATE BROWNIES

>Makes 9   >Preparation time: 1¼ hours   >Cooking time: 25 minutes

INGREDIENTS

100 g/3½ oz unsalted butter

175 g/6 oz caster sugar

6 tbsp dark muscovado sugar

125 g/4½ oz dark chocolate

1 tbsp golden syrup

2 eggs

1 tsp chocolate or vanilla essence

100 g/3½ oz plain flour

2 tbsp cocoa powder

½ tsp baking powder

METHOD

1 Lightly grease a 20-cm/8-inch shallow square cake tin and line the base.

2 Place the butter, sugars, dark chocolate and golden syrup in a heavy-based saucepan and heat gently, stirring, until the mixture is well blended and smooth. Remove from the heat and leave to cool.

3 Beat together the eggs and flavouring. Whisk in the cooled chocolate mixture.

4 Sieve together the flour, cocoa powder and baking powder and fold carefully into the egg and chocolate mixture, using a metal spoon or a spatula.

5 Spoon the mixture into the prepared tin and bake in a preheated oven, 180°C/350°F/Gas Mark 4, for 25 minutes, or until the top is crisp and the edge of the cake is beginning to shrink away from the sides of the tin. The inside of the cake mixture will still be quite stodgy and soft to the touch.

6 Leave the cake to cool completely in the tin, then cut it into squares to serve.

CHEWY VANILLA COCONUT SQUARES

>Makes 9 >Preparation time: 1¼ hours >Cooking time: 30 minutes

INGREDIENTS

225 g/8 oz dark chocolate digestive biscuits

6 tbsp butter or margarine

175 ml/6 fl oz canned evaporated milk

1 egg, beaten

1 tsp vanilla essence

5 tsp caster sugar

50 g/1¾ oz self-raising flour, sieved

125 g/4½ oz desiccated coconut

50 g/1¾ oz dark chocolate, optional

METHOD

1 Grease a shallow 20-cm/8-inch square cake tin and line the base.

2 Crush the biscuits in a polythene bag with a rolling pin or process them in a food processor.

3 Melt the butter or margarine in a pan. Stir in the crushed biscuits until well combined.

4 Press the biscuit mixture into the base of the cake tin.

5 Beat together the evaporated milk, egg, vanilla essence and sugar until smooth. Stir in the flour and desiccated coconut. Pour over the biscuit base and level the top.

6 Bake in a preheated oven, 190°C/ 375°F/Gas Mark 5, for 30 minutes, or until the coconut topping is firm and just golden.

7 Leave to cool in the cake tin for about 5 minutes, then cut into squares. Leave to cool completely in the tin.

8 Carefully remove the squares from the tin and place them on a board. Melt the dark chocolate, if using, and drizzle it over the squares to decorate them. Leave the chocolate to set before serving.

CHOCOLATE-COATED WHEAT BISCUITS

> Makes about 20 > Preparation time: 1 hour > Cooking time: 15–20 minutes

INGREDIENTS

6 tbsp butter

100 g/3½ oz demerara sugar

1 egg

25 g/1 oz wheatgerm

125 g/4½ oz wholemeal self-raising flour

60 g/2¼ oz self-raising flour, sieved

125 g/4½ oz chocolate

METHOD

1 Lightly grease a baking tray. Beat the butter and sugar until fluffy. Add the egg and beat well. Stir in the wheatgerm and flours. Bring the mixture together with your hands.

2 Roll rounded teaspoons of the mixture into balls and place these on the prepared baking tray, spacing them well apart to allow for spreading during cooking.

3 Flatten the biscuits slightly with the prongs of a fork. Bake in a preheated oven, 180°C/350°F/Gas Mark 4, for 15–20 minutes, or until golden. Leave to cool on the tray for a few minutes before transferring to a wire rack to cool completely.

4 Melt the chocolate, then dip each biscuit in the chocolate to cover the bases and come a little way up the sides. Let the excess drip back into the bowl.

5 Place the biscuits on a sheet of baking paper and leave to set in a cool place before serving.

OAT & SESAME DROPS

> Makes 10   > Preparation time: 50 minutes   > Cooking time: 15 minutes

INGREDIENTS

4 tbsp butter

125 g/4½ oz caster sugar

1 egg, beaten

50 g/1¾ oz plain flour

½ tsp salt

½ tsp baking powder

175 g/6 oz porridge oats

125 g/4½ oz raisins

2 tbsp sesame seeds

METHOD

1 Lightly grease 2 baking trays.

2 In a large mixing bowl, cream together the butter and sugar until light and fluffy.

3 Add the beaten egg gradually and beat until well combined.

4 Sieve the flour, salt and baking powder into the creamed mixture. Mix well.

5 Add the porridge oats, raisins and sesame seeds and mix together thoroughly.

6 Place spoonfuls of the mixture well apart on the prepared baking trays and flatten them slightly with the back of a spoon.

7 Bake in a preheated oven, 180°C/350°F/Gas Mark 4, for 15 minutes.

8 Leave the biscuits to cool slightly on the baking trays, then transfer them to a wire rack and leave to cool completely before serving.

FROSTED ORANGE BISCUITS

>Makes about 30 >Preparation time: 55 minutes >Cooking time: 10–12 minutes

INGREDIENTS

6 tbsp butter, softened

75 g/2¾ oz caster sugar

1 egg

1 tbsp milk

225 g/8 oz plain flour

25 g/1 oz cocoa powder

ICING

175 g/6 oz icing sugar, sifted

3 tbsp orange juice

a little dark chocolate, melted

METHOD

1 Carefully line 2 baking trays with sheets of baking paper.

2 Beat together the butter and sugar until light and fluffy. Beat in the egg and milk until well combined. Sift together the flour and cocoa powder and gradually mix together to form a soft dough. Use your fingers to incorporate the last of the flour and bring the dough together.

3 Roll out the dough on to a lightly floured surface until 5 mm/¼ inch thick. Using a 5-cm/2-inch fluted round cutter, cut out as many biscuits as you can. Re-roll the dough trimmings and cut out more biscuits.

4 Place the biscuits on the lined baking trays and bake in a preheated oven, 180°C/350°F/Gas Mark 4, for 10–12 minutes, or until golden.

5 Leave the biscuits to cool on the baking trays for a few minutes, then transfer to a wire rack to cool completely.

6 To make the icing, place the icing sugar in a bowl and stir in enough orange juice to form a thin icing that will coat the back of a spoon. Spread the icing over the biscuits and leave to set. Drizzle with melted chocolate. Leave the chocolate to set before serving.

ORANGE GINGERNUTS

> Makes about 30 > Preparation time: 25 minutes > Cooking time: 15–20 minutes

INGREDIENTS

350 g/12 oz self-raising flour

pinch of salt

200 g/7 oz caster sugar

1 tbsp ground ginger

1 tsp bicarbonate of soda

125 g/4½ oz butter

75 g/2¾ oz golden syrup

1 egg, beaten

1 tsp grated orange rind

METHOD

1 Lightly grease several baking trays.

2 Sieve the flour, salt, sugar, ginger and bicarbonate of soda into a large mixing bowl.

3 Heat the butter and golden syrup together in a saucepan over a very low heat until the butter has melted.

4 Leave the butter mixture to cool slightly, then pour it on to the dry ingredients.

5 Add the egg and orange rind and mix together thoroughly.

6 Using your hands, carefully shape the dough into 30 even-sized balls.

7 Place the balls well apart on the prepared baking trays, then flatten them slightly with your fingers.

8 Bake in a preheated oven, 160°C/325°F/Gas Mark 3, for 15–20 minutes, then transfer them to a wire rack to cool.

MIXED FRUIT CRESCENTS

>Makes about 25   >Preparation time: 35 minutes   >Cooking time: 12–15 minutes

INGREDIENTS

100 g/3½ oz butter, softened

75 g/2¾ oz caster sugar

1 egg, separated

200 g/7 oz plain flour

grated rind of 1 orange

grated rind of 1 lemon

grated rind of 1 lime

2–3 tbsp orange juice

caster sugar, for sprinkling (optional)

METHOD

1 Lightly grease 2 baking trays.

2 In a mixing bowl, cream together the butter and sugar until light and fluffy, then gradually beat in the egg yolk.

3 Sieve the flour into the creamed mixture and mix until evenly combined. Add the orange, lemon and lime rinds, and enough orange juice to make the mixture into a soft dough.

4 Roll out the dough on a lightly floured surface. Stamp out rounds using a 7.5-cm/ 3-inch biscuit cutter. Make crescent shapes by cutting away a quarter of each round. Re-roll the trimmings to make about 25 crescents.

5 Place the crescent shapes on to the prepared baking trays. Prick the surface of each crescent with a fork.

6 Lightly whisk the egg white in a small bowl and brush it over the biscuits. Dust with extra caster sugar, if using.

7 Bake in a preheated oven, 200°C/400°F/Gas Mark 6, for 12–15 minutes. Leave the biscuits to cool on a wire rack before serving.

DRY ALMOND BISCUITS

>Makes 16   >Preparation time: 55 minutes   >Cooking time: 30–40 minutes

INGREDIENTS

1 egg

100 g/3½ oz caster sugar

1 tsp vanilla essence

125 g/4½ oz plain flour

½ tsp baking powder

1 tsp ground cinnamon

50 g/1¾ oz dark chocolate, roughly chopped

50 g/1¾ oz toasted flaked almonds

50 g/1¾ oz pine kernels

METHOD

1 Grease a large baking tray.

2 Whisk the egg, sugar and vanilla essence in a mixing bowl with an electric mixer until it is thick and pale – ribbons of mixture should trail from the whisk as you lift it.

3 Sieve the flour, baking powder and cinnamon into a separate bowl, then sieve into the egg mixture and fold in gently. Stir in the chocolate, almonds and pine kernels.

4 Turn out on to a lightly floured surface and shape into a flat log about 23 cm/9 inches long and 1.5 cm/¾ inch wide. Transfer to the prepared baking tray.

5 Bake in a preheated oven, 180°C/350°F/Gas Mark 4, for 20–25 minutes, or until golden. Remove from the oven and leave to cool for 5 minutes, or until firm.

6 Transfer the log to a cutting board. Using a serrated bread knife, cut the log on the diagonal into slices about 1 cm/½ inch thick and arrange them on the baking tray. Cook for 10–15 minutes, turning halfway through the cooking time.

7 Leave to cool for about 5 minutes, then transfer to a wire rack to cool completely.

SPICED RUM BISCUITS

>Makes about 24   >Preparation time: 15 minutes   >Cooking time: 10–12 minutes

INGREDIENTS

175 g/6 oz unsalted butter

175 g/6 oz dark muscovado sugar

225 g/8 oz plain flour

pinch of salt

½ tsp bicarbonate of soda

1 tsp ground cinnamon

¼ tsp ground coriander

½ tsp ground nutmeg

¼ tsp ground cloves

2 tbsp dark rum

METHOD

1 Lightly grease 2 baking trays.

2 Cream together the butter and sugar and whisk until light and fluffy.

3 Sieve the flour, salt, bicarbonate of soda, cinnamon, coriander, nutmeg and cloves into the creamed mixture.

4 Stir the dark rum into the mixture.

5 Using 2 teaspoons, put small mounds of the mixture on to the baking trays, placing them 7.5 cm/3 inches apart to allow for spreading during cooking. Flatten each one slightly with the back of a spoon.

6 Bake in a preheated oven, 180°C/350°F/Gas Mark 4, for 10–12 minutes until golden.

7 Leave the biscuits to cool and crispen on wire racks before serving.

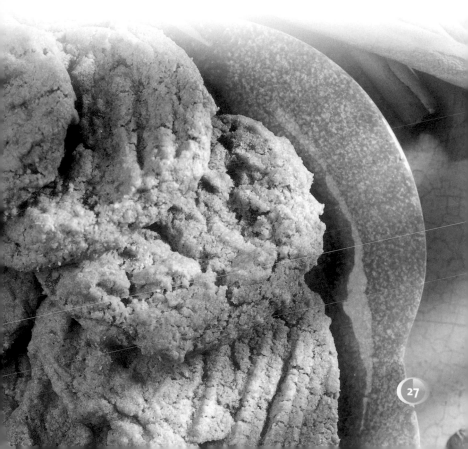

CRUNCHY PEANUT BISCUITS

>Makes 20   >Preparation time: 40 minutes   >Cooking time: 15 minutes

INGREDIENTS

125 g/4½ oz butter, softened

150 g/5½ oz chunky peanut butter

225 g/8 oz granulated sugar

1 egg, lightly beaten

150 g/5½ oz plain flour

½ tsp baking powder

pinch of salt

75 g/2¾ oz unsalted natural peanuts, chopped

METHOD

1 Lightly grease 2 baking trays.

2 In a large mixing bowl, beat together the butter and peanut butter.

3 Gradually add the sugar and beat well.

4 Add the beaten egg to the mixture, a little at a time, until it is thoroughly combined.

5 Sieve the flour, baking powder and salt into the peanut butter mixture.

6 Add the peanuts and bring all of the ingredients together to form a soft dough. Wrap and leave to chill for about 30 minutes.

7 Form the dough into 20 balls and place them on to the prepared baking trays about 5 cm/ 2 inches apart to allow for spreading during cooking. Flatten them slightly with your hand.

8 Bake in a preheated oven, 190°C/375°F/Gas Mark 5, for 15 minutes, until golden. Transfer the biscuits to a wire rack and leave to cool.

LEMON CHOCOLATE PINWHEELS

>Makes 40   >Preparation time: 1 hour   >Cooking time: 10–12 minutes

INGREDIENTS

175 g/6 oz butter, softened, plus extra for greasing

300 g/10½ oz caster sugar

1 egg, beaten

350 g/12 oz plain flour, plus extra for dusting

25 g/1 oz dark chocolate, melted and cooled slightly

grated rind of 1 lemon

METHOD

1 Grease several baking trays lightly, and dust them with flour.

2 In a large mixing bowl, cream together the butter and sugar until light and fluffy.

3 Gradually add the beaten egg to the creamed mixture, beating thoroughly.

4 Sift the flour into the creamed mixture and mix thoroughly until a soft dough forms.

5 Transfer half of the dough to another bowl and then beat in the cooled melted chocolate.

6 Stir the grated lemon rind into the other half of the plain dough.

7 On a lightly floured surface, roll out the 2 pieces of dough to form rectangles of the same size.

8 Lay the lemon dough on top of the chocolate dough. Roll up the dough tightly into a sausage shape, using a sheet of baking paper to guide you. Leave the dough to chill in the refrigerator until firm enough to slice.

9 Cut the roll into about 40 slices, place them on the prepared baking trays and bake in a preheated oven, 190°C/375°F/Gas Mark 5, for 10–12 minutes or until lightly golden. Transfer the pinwheels to a wire rack and leave to cool completely before serving.

SAVOURY CURRIED BISCUITS

>Makes 40 >Preparation time: 35 minutes >Cooking time: 10–15 minutes

INGREDIENTS

100 g/3½ oz butter, diced and softened, plus extra for greasing

100 g/3½ oz plain flour

1 tsp salt

2 tsp curry powder

100 g/3½ oz Cheshire cheese, grated

100 g/3½ oz Parmesan cheese, freshly grated

METHOD

1 Grease several baking trays lightly with a little butter.

2 Sift the plain flour and salt into a large mixing bowl.

3 Stir in the curry powder and the grated Cheshire and Parmesan cheeses. Rub in the softened butter with your fingertips until the mixture comes together to form a soft dough.

4 On a lightly floured surface, roll out the dough thinly into a rectangle.

5 Using a round 5-cm/2-inch biscuit cutter, cut out 40 biscuits.

6 Arrange the biscuit rounds on the prepared baking trays.

7 Bake the biscuits in a preheated oven, 180°C/350°F/Gas Mark 4, for 10–15 minutes until deep golden.

8 Leave the biscuits to cool slightly on the baking trays. Then transfer them carefully to a wire rack and leave them until they are completely cold and crisp before serving them.

SUGARED LEMON BISCUITS

>Makes about 50   >Preparation time: 25 minutes   >Cooking time: 15–20 minutes

INGREDIENTS

100 g/3½ oz butter, softened

125 g/4½ oz caster sugar

grated rind of 1 lemon

1 egg, beaten

4 tbsp lemon juice

350 g/12 oz plain flour

1 tsp baking powder

1 tbsp milk

icing sugar, for dredging

METHOD

1 Lightly grease several baking trays.

2 In a mixing bowl, cream together the butter, sugar and lemon rind until pale and fluffy.

3 Add the beaten egg and lemon juice a little at a time, beating well after each addition.

4 Sieve the flour and baking powder into the creamed mixture and blend together. Add the milk, mixing to form a dough.

5 Turn the dough out on to a lightly floured work surface and divide into about 50 even-sized pieces.

6 Roll each piece into a sausage shape with your hands and twist in the middle to make an 'S' shape.

7 Place on the prepared baking trays and bake in a preheated oven, 160°C/325°F/Gas Mark 3, for 15–20 minutes. Leave to cool completely on a wire rack. Dredge with icing sugar to serve.

INDEX